RECKLESS WOMEN

BY THE SAME AUTHOR

POETRY
the least you can do is sing, Longspoon, 1982

Songs Like White Apples Tasted, Bayeux Arts, 1998

And Still I Hear Her Singing, Touchwood, 2000

FICTION
Breakaway, Macmillan, 1974

The Nefertiti Look, Thistledown, 1987

The Love Song of Romeo Paquette, Thistledown, 1990

Salamander Moon, Snowapple, 1997

The Prisoner of Cage Farm, University of Calgary Press, 2003

NON-FICTION
Phyllis Webb: An Annotated Bibliography in

The Annotated Bibliography of Canada's Major Authors

Series, ECW Press, 1985

RADIO PLAY
The Dinosaur Connection, CBC Vanishing Point, 1988

reckless women

Cecelia Frey

RONSDALE PRESS

RONSDALE PRESS
3350 West 21st Avenue
Vancouver, B.C., Canada V6S 1G7
www.ronsdalepress.com

Typesetting: Julie Cochrane, in New Baskerville 11 pt on 13.5
Cover Design: Julie Cochrane
Cover Photo: Doane Gregory
Author Photo: Dave Brown
Paper: Ancient Forest Friendly Rolland "Enviro" — 100% post-consumer waste, totally chlorine-free and acid-free

Ronsdale Press wishes to thank the Canada Council for the Arts, the Government of Canada through the Book Publishing Industry Development Program (BPIDP), and the Province of British Columbia through the British Columbia Arts Council for their support of its publishing program.

Library and Archives Canada Cataloguing in Publication

Frey, Cecelia
    Reckless women / Cecelia Frey.

Poems.
ISBN 1-55380-017-6

    I. Title.

PS8561.R48R42 2004   C811'.54   C2004-903309-3

At Ronsdale Press we are committed to protecting the environment. To this end we are working with Markets Initiative (www.oldgrowthfree.com) and printers to phase out our use of paper produced from ancient forests. This book is one step towards that goal.

Printed in Canada by AGMV Marquis, Quebec

CONTENTS

ACKNOWLEDGEMENTS

Some of these poems, or versions of them, have been published in *blue buffalo, Camrose Review, Contemporary Verse 2, CV II, Descant, Grain, Malahat Review, NeWest Review, Pierian Spring, Poetry Canada Review, Poetry Toronto, Sanscrit,* and *Secrets from the Orange Couch.* Some were included in *Writing on the Wall,* a Women's Television Network project. "Women" and "Sexing Squash at Midnight," were performed at Womanstrength: Celebration of Women in the Arts at the Yardbird Suite in Edmonton and subsequently broadcast on CBC Radio.

I'd like to thank Christopher Frey, Catherine Fuller, Carl Svoboda and, especially, Hector Williamson for their suggestions during the writing of this collection. A further and special thanks must go to Catherine for her advice during the editing process and to Ronald Hatch for his keen eye and encouragement.

PART ONE

–

BONE ROOTS SHUDDER
OUR FEET

One returns to the self as
if to an old house . . .

– Pablo Neruda, *The Sea and the Bells*

Brown feathers

i remember morning the day i was born
they cut down the cherry tree outside my mother's window
i remember a sparrow falling
blossoms floating
          pink and white stars

a galaxy and in it a small brown house
perches, its wood alive and deep as feathers

inside the house my mother sits
looking out the window
her hands hold the walls of her belly
big as a house on her lap

and inside this
feather-soft flesh
i breathe to the rhythm of my mother

she is neither sad nor happy
she holds this nesting moment
a fragile suspension
she is listening to the earth
to the sun-spinning spiders
she is listening to feathers
pulsing wild hearts

My mother sings

lalalalala lalalalala
       lalalalala
lala

call of the lala
when blind as a kitten
raising soft paws
from its cardboard nest
behind the cookstove

child spirit calls
for a word
to cover its nakedness

lala is round
lala is soft
lala is fluid
lala is flesh
lala is patient
the form fills
empties, shrinks
shrivels, fills again
yet remains the same
knows beauty is decay
as well as green
budding and bursting

knows beauty is bone
knobbling the ground
we learn to walk

bone roots that shudder our feet
tender as peeled grapes

Taffeta ribbons

Translation of shadow into *leaf*
is to be broken
Broken is loneliness launched on its journey
Translation of spirit into child:

                      soft spot closes
                  skull shapes
                bones set

To return to the beginning of telling lies:

Shadows in the morning on the white wall
bounce
        the child opens her eyes in the quiet house
her eyes watch the warm sea's
float and drift
its creatures' sudden dart

She grows and learns it is a tree
or leaf of tree outside her window
and the word pops from her mouth

Choosing loss:
        branch is a straight line curved
        is wind dancing
        is cupped hand
                lifting
                    green air
      or hook

The mother points to
                    a movement
                    rise and fall
some thing
            dark
crosses the floor
from cookstove to door:
                    black ribbon
                    undulating rhythm or
furry mat with soft pads slinking or . . .

cat
the child echoes
the mother smiles
her front tooth is large and white
not large
but large beside others
not white
but whiter than her red lips
not really red
pink, a certain shade of pink
what some people call pink

The child mirrors the mother's smile
her finger traces
the woman mouth
curve of flesh on bone

Woman with child on hip

Balanced in a curve
because of the child
who rides her hip all summer

solid she stands
before her house
her feet planted
as young trees

She squints into the sun
into the faces of three men
strangers with black barbs
sprouting wire sharp on craterous skin
a sour smell and growls
rolling from their throats

Her voice is naked
it cannot find a place to hide
it trembles on the edge
of three million years

The child opens her mouth
her cry startles the air
nothing will comfort her
neither the mother's song
nor the smiles of men
not the mother's smile
the child knows
a false smile

Around the corral fence comes the father
wiping his hands on his coveralls.
He, too, is smiling
his voice speaks welcome
he puts out his hand
The mother smiles a different smile
The child watches the men
They paw circles in the dirt
smoke curls from their bent fingers

Peeling sticks in a wood pile

the loneliness of north
a clearing in the bush
damp after rain
late August and evening chill
in the steel light just before bedtime
the bark lifts like an impetigo scab

to clean new skin
so smooth so smooth
the cool feel of green wood
shapes an instinct, a longing for
something known and unremembered

thick gluey rivulets
curl like slug slime on the upper lip
of a scowling child
when swiped with a rough woollen sleeve
leave a silver arc
glistening
on the fresh curve of her cheek
like traces of the new moon
already rising in the east

Sitting

As we were
seven girls in summer dresses
field flowers on tangled grass

or plump brown berries all on one stem
without blemish, perfectly formed
we knew how to sit

our knees touch the earth
our fingers cradle each other
our lips are closed
nothing is lost in translation

Your leg across mine
appears artless in its placement
our intertwined arms
I cannot tell one from the other

We are looking in the same direction
at the photographer
our mother

she appears in the photograph as a shape
stout legs tapering to crown
double-trunked mountain pine
thick-rooted ever green

Silk stockings

early spring on a north road
a rut between two lines
of trees like stumps of black teeth
a trap baited
waiting
taut on the spring

dad's old wagon a jolt
a mighty screech of rusted nails
each lurch of our plowhorse team
crow claws raking a chalkboard sky

In the distance
something moves
wild cat? giant raven?
only an old woman
from the reservation
she wears a cloth
like a skirt
and on her head a cap
flap-ears down

(my child's mind busy
stories of women around the kitchen
my mother's whispers
they scar themselves at death
of husbands and sons
my aunt the nurse's confirmation
they slit their legs
with long knives

big ears me
in the corner with granny
her stick legs
banded as bird's
with droopy old woman stockings
her quick blade
slicing down skin
gouging out spud eyes)

My father ripples the reins
across our horses
their broad polished rumps
roll toward my fate
as we pass the woman
        my parents do not look
it's not polite to stare
I smell woodsmoke
damp chill, deep forest
the rawness of other

On the front seat
my mother's frills
like curtains peeping
through her jacket
the same colour as her skirt
her hat, its flower falling
across one eye

The train that will take her away
streaks through my mind
City is a word
I do not understand
already I want my mother
her sweet-smelling arms
her silk stockings rustling
like new poplar
spring mornings

Woman without breasts

Grandmother is beak
pecking on wood/tree/flesh
is claw curved on bark/bone
carried by wind
set here
out of place
to be old woman/crone

She never meant it to happen:
thoughtless of age
a young woman
leans toward the camera
chin in hand
hand/chin/cheek all round and soft

As she came into her bony authority
she forgot how once
she waited on young men

split herself six ways for sons

Female flesh, sapling green
supple and bending
she names frivolous

For her the girl child sings
like a bird
mimics
raucous caw of crow
magpie gusto

Birth of sacrifice

Winter comes
pares bones clean

With sharp nails grandmother
whittles chicken joints
sheathes her claws
to stuff my always open mouth
with flesh once alive
once throbbing, fattening for the kill

A northern child sees
trees feed winter their flesh
stripped fingers upstretched
mice and gophers offer their quivering
skeletons from wood pile to moon

I am grandchild
and the old woman takes care of me
but I have watched her cast spells
on heads paralyzed across the block
I have seen eyes like black glass waiting
her fluent art of blade

Gulls at plough time

This cut earth
shudders
in sunlight like
an open wound

Smelling it on the wind
the flocks come
They lift and swoop around and around
thick as snow
Fierce beaks carry
into the tall air
soft wingless bodies

Granny in her apron stands
looking up
curved talon
shading her eyes
She will plant the seed fairly
one pea to rot
one to mutate
one for the birds
one to grow

I move with her into summer
as with her thin flat blade
she hills potatoes
cracks the surface
of sun-baked mounds, hive
or weevil abode
lops off weed heads
helps dad slice back hide
on our milk cow's flank
clean out a nest of wobble flies
pour on disinfectant
her old woman's face stone
at poor Bess's twitch of muscle

In the lantern's thin light
I watch a pouch of loose skin beneath her chin
as she swallows fish like a pelican
Yet I collaborate in nature's atrocities
Grandmother
lancing a green-pus boil
on my white and tender thigh

Hair washing day

When prairie speaks most evil
late winter afternoon
when prairie howls
I kneel
place my head on the block
squeeze my eyes tight

Black carries me down
down to bottomless pit
down to still water
down to drowning

Claws pinch and press until the sap runs clear
Screams rise
burst from my throat
like pricked blisters
dribble down my shift front
trickle to broken words

Before the black-fired oven
a trophy
my scalp wrapped in a towel
safe for another week
while granny toasts bread
to dunk in chocolate

The dilemma
how not to love this monster
life-giver
    life-taker
how to leave

To feel at home in this place
is to have an instinct for death
my mother's silent terror
of the dark and cold and uncontrolled fire
and my father
attempting circumvention of his fate
stopping a moment on the cliff edge
crippled and blinded
before taking flight
to keep his appointment in Samarra

Rain

Rain is raining all around

rain on car windows
leaving
rain on child's hand
drawing circles in the mist
on child's eye centred

Rain comes between the eye
and the brown house
Rain separates
fence, barn, woodpile
where we sat
in the cold rain

Rain cuts across faces
aunts who came
bearing brimming pots
filling kitchens with words
with yeast sprouting
in every nook and corner
foam flowering on the bowl's rim

and uncles who could hear the rain's slant
at calf time they came
bearing their hairy arms
like soft brushes
hiding in their blunt hands
blades
bottles smelling of pine
kneeling in red hay, their bent heads
listening to rain

Rain falls on graves of mothers
gumbo that would pull me in
spread its blanket across my face
thicker even than the rain

On the road to Athabasca

All the beautiful things
go into the muskeg

Faces of beloveds
float an instant
like white lilies they open
close and are sucked backwards

People with mythologies know how to approach death
having experienced so much of it
Romancing the bog
they contrive heroes
with missions
of descent

And so my angels
lie in wait
gathering strength
until full circle come
out of the deep alive

In this enchanted place
they rise to possess me
I become a mother weeping
an old woman raging against the night

Visiting ice caves at Bragg Creek

Consider first the tree:
to dissolve through scars
stretched to new growth
to juice swelling
the sappy green

To penetrate the flesh layer
whirl through rings of years
down to fingers
that can crack stone

To travel underground tunnels
creating their own space
in search of food
To nuzzle earth, again
become seed

Consider prairie as echo
of hollow the primitive mind knows
feeling its own absence
threading backward
instructed to keep
to carry egg
egg's shell, its fragility
through a long and precarious night

Prairie child without a mirror
is rain, is wind, is coyote howl
is dog curled behind stove
is sister, brother
Without her own
takes language
as she finds it

The flashlight trembles in my hand
so violently it falls
rolls into deep dark
I hear it echo back and down
its small light disappears into the earth's core
A star blinks for an instant in the night sky

Sweet smoke

i.

The new sidewalks in town

cat's footprints
caught airy nothing
sliding sleekly through night
her journey recorded
forever in asphalt

Did she puzzle at the
once familiar ground
beneath her feet?
lift one paw
pink tongue curling
on bitter tar?

ii.

Boardwalks
pungent with new spruce
echo first high heels
                    tripping
to the Saturday night dance

Young girls
step high as cranes
in cattail marshes
tremble as hollow rushes
in a light wind
vibrate as fiddles
suspended on a high note

Fearful of not being asked
of being asked
we moved to music
closer than we knew

iii.

Planks set across gumbo
broad as vistas
opening in exotic lands

Women silent as moccasins
walking in damp leaves
dark as deep woods
remote as roads without signs

I squeeze my mother's hand

When we are safe I dare
a backward look
a cat stiffens on a porch rail
leaps softly
into the tall grass

The solemn house

During the war no one was allowed to speak
while the six o'clock news was on
an old couple lived next door in a large white house
a pretty lady lived across the lane, her husband
was in a mine sweeper in the north Atlantic
my father was upstairs dying in his bed

Once the lady crossed the lane
she and my mother
played the piano and sang songs
that were not hymns
how their voices rang out
startling everyone

When my father was having a good day
we sat with him on the horsehair sofa
sometimes we sat on his knee
while he read to us the Sunday coloureds

My uncle came from far away
he wore a uniform and smoked
he would take a drink
he had girlfriends
all this seemed very strange

It was there I started school, about which
I remember nothing significant
but I remember Allen's where we bought jelly beans
with a nickel, I remember the tidy glass bins
and especially the black licorice pipes
tipped with beads of fire

And Terrabain's where my younger sister
tried to buy a candy with a penny
which had passed through her digestive tract

No other children were in the neighbourhood
except a boy named Tony
who chased me and threw rocks
one day for refuge I ran to the nice lady's porch
Tony's rock broke a full milk bottle
he ran off and *I* got the bawling out

I slept upstairs with granny who kept
gingersnaps and peppermints under her pillow
to ward off collywobbles in the night
we pulled the covers over our heads
to keep out dangerous air
In summer when heat gathered in the rooms
we slept on the verandah
under a canopy of mosquito netting
I imagined was a sultan's tent

PART TWO

—

EYES BURNING
THROUGH STONE

Silence is intensified
into a stone

– Pablo Neruda, "XIX," *Stones of the Sky*

The woman who lost herself
in the process of stone

How did we by chance arrive in that stone village
where even the postcards were pale
the tea shop windows slippery smooth
their granite glare watching the square, the sea-bleached
green and duck pond
                stone water's leap

What propelled us to a savage coast
    a stone house set apart
what steered us to the doorway
of a woman
exile in her husband's country
Her face/my face
startled me more than barking dogs

Looking ten years back, I hold in my hand
a salt-scoured scene, beyond quiet as if
quiet were a thing of degree and stillness, too.
The image transfixes: lace curtains
and behind them eyes
             and ears disapproving
our destruction of their silence
our rented car, its jackhammer sound
ripping up their ancient cobbles

as brashly, with a burst of petrol
we crest
take a perilous turn
onto a desolate approach
leading to her, eyes
                burning through stone
their fierce speaking
of a life lived
outside her own language
each night of every year
inserting herself
between a stranger's stone sheets

Molly's marmalade

Dark with a wild taste.
Think Seville, flamenco dancers
their flared orange skirts
sculpted to knife edge
a controlled art yet with
the appearance of abandon
like Molly's eyebrows
winging thick and black
her hair, its bramble tangles

Around the barn edge she comes
silencing the dogs
her own silence turbulent
as the furrows of her brow
sharp as her switchblade eyes
We bend to cross her threshold
beneath stones that stand
exactly arched
how many centuries ago
by what unknown craftsman

Home comfort on the sea coast
the directory read
Our eyes climb walls
tall as ravaged cliffs
probe ceiling plaster
clotted as loose clouds
(I hope for hot water in the bathroom
my sceptical companion hopes for a bathroom)

At breakfast we learn we are
her only guests
in a long while
not a good season for visitors
perhaps it is the weather
the rate of exchange
perhaps this is, I whisper
a place too real for tourists

From out the back
black cauldron bubbles
umber's glug and spit
struts its bitter perfume
pip, pulp, peel, white rind

Marmalade busily becoming
reassures us
Molly is an ordinary woman
housewife tending her kitchen
as she sets before us pots of tea
and toast rack, why do I sense windigo
heart full of bitter desire, or undine
childless and longing for the impossible

The sea cliff hike

I walk this strange path and wonder
where I have seen it before
this pasture, these cows raising ponderous heads
belling the morning dew
their glazed eyes
focused on the slow process of cud

With one difference
here fences are electric
and red signs warn of dangers
of entering unknown territory

To arrive on this shark-tooth point
to stand against the wind
be whittled to bone
to stare down
into the churning
foam-topped chop

Yet it is not the sea turns me queasy
nor the plunging cliffside
nor fierce whips lashing granite

but the woman's strange familiar voice
demanding *leap*
leap her raspy sigh rises
out of the shark's throat

Greater horseshoe bat

To your cave in the heartland
without maps or even one sign
I come bearing my ignorance
proudly like frankincense and myrrh

by accident discover your plaque
rivetted in stone
endangered species, this cage
is for her own good

In her long wintering out
hoarfrost may form on her pelt
she can hold sperm all winter
she will cultivate it in spring

I spread myself against your bars
narrow my eyes into your dark
after a long while I see nothing

only at my shoulder something
stirs, a black wind
blows cool across my nape
spiny fingers tangle in my hair

The old woman and the stile

Here they provide passage from one field to another
neighbourly steps for an easy crossing

A country of walkers
grannies stride in seven league boots
small children show off
miniature brogues with red laces

This is a country you can feel
through the soles of your shoes, your feet
tingle with the bones of its heroes
stirring in their shallow graves

Your eyes flicker with the green flame
of grass, your ear hums
with the music of footsteps
your wide-open arms
gather this country like ripe sheaves

This is my grandparents' place
I walk its roads and sea coasts
accompanied by gods and ghosts
and in travelling backwards to find myself
recall an uncle's story:
grandmother for the first time walking
into her new home on the prairie, tears
streaming from her eyes

Having just arrived
from across the North Atlantic
across three thousand miles of earth
clenched in winter's savage fist
Ice wind scything down from tundra
threatening the CN line
the only passage, steel rails
This new world
calling for a merciful god who will not come,
the bones of its heroes in frozen ground

Fence building

The old country is plotted with stones, built
on the patience of men who stacked them here
centuries of piling rock upon rock
through wars and occasional times
of peace, stubbornly building fences

Instinct placed the first stone
then balancing it, the second
until the first small circle was rounded
and the man squatted back on his haunches
grunting satisfaction

or, woman
this impulse
from bog and granite coast
to quilt earth patches
to stake a claim
For I recall the summer
Elnore and I built a fence
between our two properties
and how, to catch and preserve the sun
in the resilient pores of our skin
we wore our bikinis

I held the board to the crossbar
secured on stout uprights
She struck the blows
in a series of near hits
hammer glancing nail heart
over and over
our sound trembled out
like water-skipping pebbles

starting ripples that circle back
twenty years or more
when with breasts,
round and smooth and firm as stones
nested in bright slings,
we took on the summer laughing

The home place

Where imagination doves the air
lights in every rickety Dublin loft and corner
where the grey swoop of evening
capes my shoulders
I pace crumbling sidewalks
to find myself

where grandmother is girl again
buttoned-up young wife
I trace her daily round: draper
greengrocer, butcher. We share
the mingled smells of blood and sawdust

Just off O'Connell street
cat in window draws me through
the weathered frame
my reflection in lace pattern
cat yawns and my mouth opens
cat flicks her whiskers
grandmother's chin wobbles

in a prairie garden

sweet-peas in tangles of disorder
riots of rainbow arches
hurdle wire fences
cat stalks robin in the trenches
between parsnip shawl and rhubarb flounces
and grandmother, curved gnome
and I, child again
doing the rounds with granny
the butcher's glob of red on white
pencil stuck behind his ear, straw hat

a tourniquet plumping his brow
like sausage in casing
Free liver for the cat

I still walk sidewalks
where the sun bakes mud to clay
calls to mind those far-off summers:
an old woman carved to fit the new place
where carrion eater perches on skull
my child's hand caught
in speckled talons

Terracotta statuettes, 2nd Century C.E.

Mother goddess in basket work chair nursing a child
Group of three: Celtic mother goddesses seated with
fruit (fertility symbol) in lap

lips closed and half smiling
as if they know a secret
mute to the accusation
in the matter of their sex

prepared as though
with trimmed lamps
holding the pelvic tilt
the taut artistic stance

they never go slack
shake off their sculpted aloofness
stir out of their deep reluctance
defend themselves to themselves

a full gallery in the British Museum
devoted to an attitude cast in stone:
we made the story happen
Eve ate the apple
Mary birthed the boy child

Sighting in the Munich museum

Shuffling through the Old Masters
all that burgundy, burnt sienna, cobalt blue
layers laid on with palette knife
those acres of skin
kilos of lolling flesh on hot velvet
a bevy of bursting breasts
and the young couple before me
illicitly eating peaches
kiss through peach-sweet lips

The young walk in crowds thick as tourists
through air heavy with sizzling *Bratwurst*
they consume miles of *Strudel* without worry
Schlagsahne oozing through lean brown fingers
they swing their backpacks so lightly
weightless as the sun on their shoulders

      wheel their bicycles into the Marienplatz
raise their eyes as children
to the ancient tower
glockenspiel
duel of knights
the white and shining and the black
plumed horses, a perfect ritual of lances
until the last dancing bear winds down

Light as thin boned birds
they glide in an upward draft
In innocent forests
they unroll their beds
drink from clear mountain springs
At morning
their wheels will spin new roads
to shape their flight
tonight with her tongue she licks
nectar from his laughing mouth

Hats in shop window

The way through yellow glass is long and hard.

An empty square baking in August sun
turning around the window with its straws
wide-brimmed and purple-ribboned
its satins tall and white-feathered, elegant
aristocratic old-fashioned birds, red berries
protected by yellow glass.

Yellow glass is strange to me
and yet familiar. I know it from the past
although we did not have it on the prairie
The hats, too, are of another time and place
as is the black-haired woman, her regal bearing
her pompadour, her dark eyes snapping,
who waits in her stifling room recounting betrayals
chanting revenge, who lines her walls
with words, believing them
the best defence against eyes circling like wolves.

Yellow glass in a foreign city
returns me to hats and the woman
in her stifling room, her connection with the mother at home
who had no words for betrayal or vengeance
only a thin pinched face
while her daughter stood in the open doorway
extracting payment for her life

And the prophecy of red eyes weeping
closes its yellow translucence around me.

PART THREE

—

AQUABELLE IN
THE SUBURBS

The woman struggles to lift the brimming urn
Before the mouth is sealed and all's interred

– Nancy Holmes, "Keats and the Nectarine"
from *The Adultery Poems*

Women

for Gail Harris

Women in pyjamas, women in lace
looking across their shoulders
women with tangled hair
women in kitchens creating magic
with leftovers
women with frizzed hair, women in hats
women in veils, women
in baby dolls giving the eye to
men who flip through their pages.
Women in sweatsuits pumping iron
women pushing strollers through the zoo
women who take six kids
their own and the neighbours' to see
women in fatigues and work boots pulling weeds
women with tanned arms taking tickets
at cages, women answering questions: why
does the orangutan search her baby's ear? why
when she finds fleas does she eat them? what
are those things that hang to her belly?
                              Women with flawed voices
singing the blues, women with strange accents
calling dogs in city parks.
Women in drag
women in little high heels
women with red painted toenails and cutouts
in the toes of their shoes
women with long legs and short skirts
on street corners, women with purple lips smoking
cigarettes one after another
tiny porcelain women

with transparent skin
veins pulsing like neon.
Female collectors with urns and glass jars
containing gallstones, stripped veins, withered uteri
women who houseclean and throw out glass jars
women who keep everything
and hand it down to their daughters
daughters who keep their mother's ashes on the mantle.
Women with smooth brows in sepia photographs
careless women who squint into the sun.
Women in winter rooms at dusk
picking up today's things and laying down things for tomorrow
women in children's rooms telling stories.
Women in hotel rooms
reckless women who tear off their clothes
and toss them from the balcony
and have nothing to go home in
shy women who undress beneath the blankets
in closets behind closed doors
women who believe in their cellulite thighs
their stretch marks and scars.

Women in summer dresses
women in saris, women in jeans, women
buttoned to the throat
women in long beads like ropes
women with stabbed ears
Women sitting in white chairs listening to men

the tongue fills the mouth with flesh

They sit in their cozy sunroom
discussing the dictionary
his face flinches
at her feminine logic
or lack of, the silence
between moon and man

He reminds her of *manacle*
masterful, monogamy, and
how about *mannequin*
monolingual, Mercury the winged god
and *mercy killing,* and hundreds
of mis's
I guess there is *monologue* she says

His mouth is straight-faced
at her attempt at humour, her apologies
tripping over each other, her pain
at her assault on his ears
after he was so kind to save her
from her own destruction
the least she can do
is learn his language

Daily she watches him watch
her tongue dig its own grave
turning inner to outer

watches his dancing across her scar
an old wound knit by time
circling her neck. Remembering
what it felt like
her life seeping out
she slides her finger along the rope
where the surgeon pursed the edges
where black thread dug holes

words as a second language

Oh to disown the utterance that binds us to this planet
embarrassment of the self through speech
malapropisms the least of it
doomed to attempt the gap
between what we feel
and putting it into words
we open our mouths
see what comes up
to bring that choke of shame
     scrabbling
back of the throat
exciting betrayal
saying what we do not mean
saying too much
or not enough
the ever revealing word
brands the interloper
  uninvited guest
  crashing the feast
  crying for bread
  crumbs
  anything
and why?

considering
what gets lost in translation
the distance between love
and *love*

the verb *to jump*
is not the same as feeling
both feet lifting
  at the same time
free of earth

The flood

When the water broke they were caught
in the flats looking up
toward the cliffs of the Saskatchewan
their brown shack angled and floating
a soggy teabag steeping in a brackish brine

A boat full of girls they were
adrift for several days, until
rescued by young men with motors
and carried off one by one
to higher ground

Unfamiliar with that place
they did not speak the language
mud dwellers in the upper air
yet stranded as they were
all that thrust and throttle
had its appeal

When the banks caved in
they were making fudge
an occupation involving
much of their time, being
at the precise age of addiction
Golden it tasted
of the sun, or pollen
folded into dew-moist
bell-shaped petals

In the following confusion
they lost the recipe
and though sometimes they get together
still, try different strategies
ingredients, cooking times
it never turns out the same
as they remember it. One sister grew fat
searching for that past
texture, another thin
pining
for the taste suspended
just out of reach
somewhere in the synapses

Youth and promise and each other
lost when
stirring down starbursts
glugging molten gold erupting
raw refining preciously to substance
the whole aswirl
they heard something:
split of floodgates
wrench of nail from wood

The vanilla man's lady

If he was the vanilla man
suitcase in hand
travelling these country roads
                rain rutted
                drought dusty
in his clankety jalopy
that might be named Rosinante
seeing his dark shape through the screen
she might view him with suspicion

                        knowing the stories
(salesmen who entice daughters to their beds)
she might lock the door
before his silver tongue
can dance her on its edge
spin her a conical shape
present her to strangers
as another vanilla man's lady

But what if his hands unsettle the air
        in nervous strokes
touch so brief, so light
she would not feel their sting
until he disappears
through noon light
    shimmering silver the supple willow
        bending to her window
and bathing his sweat from her body
she notices a red mark, thin as wren's claw
slitting throat to navel

What if his fingers hover
over his case lined with dark velvet
as he points out each condiment and spice
what if his mouth is dark velvet
and in the warm and closed room rises
a hum of smells like yellow coated bees
                    cinnamon striped
rind of lemon
crossed with bitter almond

The calico cat

She arrives from the night
with the moon, assembles
on the sill a moment
then leaps into the edge of his words
(he sits composing
by that lamp they bought
laughing together
at the garage sale —
shade of six laced plastic
landscapes
when the light revolves
water falls)

On her journey she is weightless
padded feet light
on his shoulder, knee, the floor
orange, yellow, grey scatter
as his eye turns
reforms her, again
she shifts on his eye's angle
gathers her colours
and disappears

Upon reflection
she is not fur, muscle, bone
She is without substance,
shape or sound
The air has opened, closed
her molecules rearranged
as absence.

Why aren't there more female magicians?

Not to know
how her tricks are done
the process
of ice
sweat
as knives quiver at throats
or scars
when she misses
or lacerations
in freeing herself
from velvet-lined boxes
and the sea of sharks
she must swim through
alone
each time

Not explanations
of smooth movement
nor theories of shadows
on screens
nor complaints
about hours of rehearsal
on midnight stages
or stories of her assistant
his smile bright as spangles
fitting locks on cages
so she can escape again

Only silver
            falling
     falling through nets
scarves
          splendiferous
               their silken sigh
                   carving the air

Only her arm's perfect arc
     and perched there
               lark
           from fire
           its white wings raised
                 singing

Journey of the sad egg

You leave your house early in the morning with the rain
endlessly sighing its green desire
the zucchini leaf spreading on the vine
you return to yellow
brittle as tobacco
the long fruit rotted at the bloom

You leave your house hoping
that someone will meet you when you get there
and pick up the tab
for the taxi
you sit on a bench in an unfamiliar station
until the slats make grooves in your back
and the janitor's bins echo in the empty hallways

You leave your house in winter for a weekend
in the country
with strangers you hope will be friends
you get off at the wrong stop
you step into snow
to the tops of your silken thighs
you watch your train leave
you listen to its whistle
fading farther and farther
into the distance
leaving you stranded in ruined shoes

Now you wait in the entry with your suitcase
packed and ready
but no one comes to take you to the station
After awhile
you return the key to its lock
you put everything back into the dusty drawers

Complaint of a jigsawed woman

Our Italian neighbours
supply us with summer diversion
                     lusty voices
fearless in battle
while we silently declare
momentary cease fire
to run around the house closing windows

In her bikini she suns on her balcony
He builds his back yard jacuzzi
She accuses him of sawing her in half
straight across the mid section she says
flinging her gestures into the air
like globules of blood

This poem is to tell her she's lucky
to live with an ordinary magician
satisfied with a plain old-fashioned saw
nothing kinky, some insist on special blades
the complications of curlicues

A woman may plan to watch from the audience
a safe distance
from singed feathers
tacky stains on taffeta
sequins hanging by a thread

then let herself be enticed
by a tongue
furling smoke
curling her toward the stage
a cunning slot
where she kneels
fits her neck
and waits
for the echo of her head
clunkety clunk down each hollow step
for the jump of severed nerve ends
dancing to a script

      mesmerized
by a smile crafty as a child
magician's, by a voice
like a superimposition on the soundtrack
this is only a trick of words and hands

Under the Louise Bridge

Lovers walk along the Bow's bend
on red shale pathways beneath leafing poplars
through honeysuckle and wolf willow
so sweet it draws bees from the suburbs
Distant children's voices pipe thin notes
and the old couple walking before us
shade themselves with a Chinese umbrella

Indifferent to the water's flash and break
or the canoe people riding the current
paddles balanced
the lovers curl themselves into each other

As they disappear into cool stone
you explain perfect arches
the elegance of mathematics
A curve of air supports tonnes of metal
ourselves in metal cages

The lovers cross the bridge
without benefit of equations, unaware
they are walking on rainbows
suspended as they are
she in the curve of his shoulder
he in a loop of her iridescent hair

Lady in blue taffeta

On the knickknack shelf she sits
with fragile soup bowls
the cracked antique jug, the peasant
in high gloss ceramic
bent beneath his load of sticks

Looking through my shape
blowsy and jagged
in perpetual process
his eyes see her
skin flawless as porcelain
lips shaped like a heart
satin hair sheening

Her wide eyes see nothing
her ears are sealed shut
while upstairs all night
I worry calamities
beneath closed lids
bombs scream and fall
and I am running without legs

This lady is someone he bought
in a mistaken moment, I said
You never like my gifts, he said

Thus we accuse each other
I view the anachronism and wonder
how long must I go on
with this nuisance to dust
                              once a week
And what if my hair takes on a sheen
What if my eyes stop seeing

I cannot toss her into the dustbin
she is both lovely and blameless
If only she would get up and go
but where could she go
in her little frock, crisp blue
her spotless white apron
her frilled housecap
her fine black slippers

not meant for the street
People in passing cars would stare
as she hesitates on the dusty curb
one foot arched into the traffic

Love as strategy

In search of a love object
they head for the mountains
She is the one driving
Beside her the wheel of his mind
stretches flesh, unpins bone

At the edge of the city
he settles into the rhythm
of his complaint
his mind in old slippers
her thought cannot follow

She can smell his fear
the sweat of his pain
She can see his fingers
move, crotch to scalp
work his yeasty veins
come to rest like hummingbirds
above his lip

She knows his need
to hear everything
from his own mouth
language as narcotic to rouse his passion
each word
glass shard
brilliant in the gut
excites him

She is a stone face
stonier than these mountains
they pass through
His words are a chisel
sculpting himself
in her layers

Woman with her throat cut

after a primitive sculpture

In this room their history
pursues them in circles
that grow smaller and smaller

The windows are painted shut

A man and a woman
the spaces between them
he fills with words
his mouth shapes anagrams
she cannot answer
graphics of forfeiture
its intricacies

On the bed their bones
awkward as rusty springs move
not with the easy rhythm
of Eden lovers
but angled
to its own spasms
each body falls alone
exhausted
each into its own skin, welded
blue and shining
to its own cold bone
falls back into
the air's worried whine

The woman draws in her limbs
her sound is small and dry
she does not flicker
an eye, one foot a tree
cannot reach the earth
one hand
        an empty cup
        a petal blown
one a claw closes on her throat

Outside the window
another woman
in her backyard sings
as she bathes her child standing
in a large tin tub
as she spreads her wash
on thin humming lines
something about morning
something about oranges

Aquabelle in the suburbs

It is the end
of a dry summer

Down a long chute
slick as a seal's back
she slips into his pool

He sips his dry martini, lights
up the barbecue and arranges his mind
regarding the awkward movements
of this strange fish
dropped from the sky
How does it find his place
to flounder, perhaps drown?

Knights are passé, it seems
postmodern damsels in distress
must perform their own rescues

Ever the plucky lass
under his gaze
she peels off her old scales
                walks on water
sculls and fins without ripple
collects points with rounded thighs
exemplary thrust and glide
        then the finale (grand if you insist):
stretching toes and fingertips
back arched on the wheel
she begins the descent

On the edge his outline dissolves
into a shimmying mix of water
and evening's golden windows
as with her new beauty
ascending
she takes all the time she needs
to describe a perfect dolphin circle

Thoughts while traversing Rogers Pass

I was born tongue-tied
cord around my neck
and stuck
the decision not mine
whether or not to turn back
from eruption into voice, the seduction
of silence so tempting.

We sit in our car in a tunnel
waiting for snow plows
hoping they are out there some place, people
in control of machines and weather
our faces white as the landscape
still as these mountains.
No one speaks
each in his own way reminded perhaps
of that first journey: a tight fit
through close walls.
Alone now as before

or accompanied even then by those who passed before?
the people we bring with us here
those doubles in old photos
in old countries, who inhabit whitewashed stone
walls of ivy thick as bushes
gardens overgrown with roses, those who
perch and precisely cross their ankles
in pale wicker, drink endless tea from cracked saucers
which I recognize
though never travelling in that country.

Would they in return
recognize their silence broken
by my birth wail? screams
of dislocation
not yet attempting harmony
but flailing protest.
Would my voice shame them
as it does me
when I catch it unaware
on a taped telephone greeting, for instance
and realize how long
the journey toward grace.

I peel back tissue and find

not the red rose
of flamenco dancers
the sun in the skin of their shoulders

not bougainvillaea
its flared skirt
a blaze of seduction

nothing of tropical gardens
where lovers sing beneath balconies
at midnight to the moon

but in the cold dark
back of the refrigerator
in pristine florist box
mint green tissue
breathing icy fragility

white gardenia, waiting

In the Crystal Palace

I am the one in plumed hat
elbow folded on table
smoke drifting through my fingers
                         winter sun rays
angling from the skylight
settle cold light
on tea, muffins
china, dazzling
white linen
women telling leaves

Late Sunday mornings
silk sheathed, wool muffled
we sought ancient ceremony
assumed an attitude
        engraved cigarette holder
        an admirer's gift
I can't remember his name

I remember faces
as though through gauze
glitter of green eye
half curve of blotted scarlet
and voices murmuring incantations
like a pale sheet rising, falling, raising
petitions heavenward

As Madame Zausz with purple hair
half-inch eyelashes, red cracked cheeks
brows raised forever surprised
portions with her pen
                exotic beaches
                the moon in our window

Shaping lovers in jagged edges
her brittle rings splinter
winter's white sun

The woman who lives in the lane

does not need a coat in winter
she keeps warm by beating her wings
so swiftly they break
the crystalline air

this same woman spring days
scrapes birds from her window
sparrows who mistake the sky
coolly cleans bits of flesh
feather from her nails

summers in her garden
with long scissors
she snips alive
rose petals

iguana

Cold blooded and unlovely she sits
on a rock in a glass case
proposing the silent riddle
of her Gioconda smile.
Yet in water
she is graceful
her body a long weave
limbs delicate
toes exquisitely pointed
proud head high.

The man who owns her
tells me she sleeps
on his hairy chest
that her skin is
soft as feathers
fine as tissue.

She is valued for flesh and eggs
he says, his fingers appraising
her meaty sides, her circling bars.
She can disappear into stone.

I stare and stare as if the muted foliage
the background sandstone grit
were a hologram
in which with a flip of vision
suddenly one fragment —
dewlap, tail tip — hooks the eye
opening the message like a flower:
inside is outside
          red leathery spine
          external eardrum
          jaw-joined teeth
          exposed unblinking eye

She is the poem
      perfect and revealed
      essence precisely defined
plated skull
crest of scales
claws that can tear skin
           like words
that have travelled a long distance to arrive.

PART FOUR

_

NOTES FROM
A HANDBAG

is it not better abort than be barren?
– Samuel Beckett, "Cascando"
from *Collected Poems in English and French*

the barrens

never so absurd
in daylight
as starlight
catching it
without warning
in half sleep
the mind sags
the eye opens
               wide
instant of
something

can't say
shadow   shape
something in the shadow of a shape
            hollow
at the sight so brief
of nothing
there

inside
in side
in   side
the head
something
some   thing
  dangling

dread yea

here I go again
shedding the old
skin the old
painful
shedding
the never ending
shedding of you
the inevitable
calling
up
the old flow
the once again
juice
each time so afraid
of loving
of not loving
enough
that you will not
leave me
that you will
strand me
in this place
terrified
of finishing
for
all
time
of not being
able
to finish

why is it I cannot say
this is the end
and stop
one day
stop
saying
without you there is no truth
no life
stop putting up with your untimely leavings
your insistent entries
stop searching beneath stones

why is it I remember and forget
over and over again
see so I may not see
not lose so I may lose
this lifetime shedding is too much

how about a new body for the waste
for the de- and re-construction
for the mis- and re-construing
the re-stewing
is it only your body can tell me
what I need to know

some love me
by forgiving me myself
you only you
could not love me
if I were other

terms of exchange

swamp out the gobbet
hang us by the heels
no matter we're blue
shivering into day
hairless as gerbils
at the starting gate
ready   set   go

steady now   and
we're   on   our   way

in for the wail
then out
everything
let it go
right to the edge
make room for more
in
        extending
heart   lungs   belly
all
plump it now
                    for out
            make room for in
that's the way
empty yourself
be filled   ·

notes from a handbag

this is no country
for dreamers
to define nothing
takes
        wit
what can you say against it

poem suffers from lack of focus

without central image
no opening
out

down hill
R turn
follow sign
2 sets lights
turn
2 sets lights
                turn

issue 61 #9 p. 36, 1995
CanLit 140/143 winter '94

Pacific Renaissance
Cedar Room 4:00–5:15

locker: 38 clockwise, once past 28
straight to 22, yellow, full size

sole or flounder — Sat. night

Call Lois

please welcome our reader

gallery possibles:
Mira Godard ritzy
Graphic small
Masters — thing in
middle of floor
contraceptive foam
Canadian maybe

poem lacks impact and energy

what this poem needs is a penis

Apple Tree road
Cherry rd.
Peggy's cove, now there's a place
you can get a grip on

cinnamomum camphora

cold camphor travel my veins
think you gonna cure me
treat my pain and fever
with your coooool rush?

where you come from camphor
you come from that upside down place?
that head-standing place?
with your scent of herbs
strong and weedy
your taste like bitter
waste places

I can see through you, camphor
    your translucent leaves
      your ephemeral wood

what you gonna do, camphor
you gonna hollow me out?
replace all that coagulated
blood with your cleeeean
                  jet stream
you gonna make the body snap

make the mind
        snap snap
look for your place all right
creep arterial tunnels
probe for brain
you gonna poison me, camphor?
you gonna explode me
with your white flowers?

dog days

this is love's end
stagnant
blood pools
stirred
now and then
by the split hoof
incantations and
midnight trysts

as Sirius rises with the sun
my poems get shorter and shorter
disappear into heat shimmer
into toad stew

i stand at the open door
of my refrigerator
cooling my toes
smelling sour
cottage cheese
think what a great metaphor
for life itself
nothing can return it to innocence

think riddled lungs
hacking up gobs
impelled to the end
to lift trillions
of trillions
of molecules. o the hours
days, years of sodden exchange
give us a rest
they have a right to say
put us on hold
upon occasion

yet
predictions for October:
once more Venus will ascend
a sky clean as mint
brisk as new love

the getaway

we move together
into rented rooms
and leave
no forwarding address
When they track us down
we escape through an open window
while they are breaking down the door

sometimes we sleep
in abandoned cars
in parks beneath trees
They accuse us of an
incestuous relationship
little do they know
survival takes all our time

we left our tricks behind
and amuse ourselves with stories
how, without us
the automatic ice maker
won't know how to stop
turning out identical cubes
how the garbage maw will starve

there, everyone was a stranger
made dangerous
by knowing too much
and understanding nothing
Here, our circle of one
spirals tighter and tighter
in our lucid moments
we admit our specific density
may become a serious problem

bloody feet and eels

after Salvador Dali

can we dream of unknown places?
one night I saw details of deserts
cliffs rising sheer
from a cloud-pale sea
putrid with sun
in the background a city
bleached
clay
brittle as finger flick

my feet wade in water twisting with eels
shock waves break my skin
along the beach
a dog with strange eyes
foams at the mouth
it bites the children's bare heels
the sand trails red

the dog, white and hairless as a grub
closes in on itself
chases its devils in circles
that become smaller
and smaller

the balloon man

the sand sparkles
it is a bright clean morning
when they pull my father out of the sea

he lies legs spread
arms eagled
lungs stones

scurf curdles his skin
is it water or sweat
or the inside's dark
                uncoiling

he asks for nothing
not air
not food
he has drunk an ecstasy of salt
his spasms are at peace
a clown balloon
collapsed, fizzled out, flat

then come the spectators
shuffling and restless as though
sensing something ominous in the air
their long shadows lash his back
their curious eyes ask
will he surface
or finish his drowning

one man kneels
positions the head
on its pillow of broken glass
another kind man breaks open
the soft shell mouth
hooks out the tongue
deft fingers section the ribs
                hold a moment
the fragile cage of my father's life
then press as though to break it

in that moment of breath suspended
                     I wonder
how many times must he bounce back up
head bobbing on the waves, must he
attach a smile to his lips
grief seeping from his eyes

and yet my feet are a link in the circle
my hands are part of the kind man's hands
I, too, insist on his pain
For us he vomits the sea

Calgary highway, March 1st

now death
dying starts

every year it's the same
sky sucked clean
of the last blizzard
trees gnawed to the bone
moon a thin trace
white on white
upper air turbulence
mottles
the land
spots of mould
mildewed quilt
stubble tufts
life at zero

people have waited it out
not willing to surrender
flesh to frozen ground
or maybe it's only a lifetime habit
this hanging on through winter

or maybe when they feel
that giant thick-furred
web-footed rodent
settle on their shoulders
squeeze round the neck
they endure because of an old promise

like the video game
we played before death entered our lives
when all possibilities were possible
and all you had to do was
click enter
take inventory
look in your knapsack and find
all the waiting people

then a summer morning
could replace these sad fields
and let me see sunrise
love
first love
why not first love
grass cool and damp
sprinklers fanning rainbows
we took off our shoes
we ran through the arches

PART FIVE .

—

SEXING SQUASH
AT MIDNIGHT

If prospects for a crop are poor due to
scarcity of bees or flowers hidden by leaves,
the diligent gardener can transfer pollen
from the male bloom to the stigma
of the female bloom.

— *The Prairie Gardener's Guide*

Definition

Labouring from dream into desire
                        becoming child
labouring to become mother
meeting at the axis

Love is recognition of the curled leaf
that grew too close to the wall
womb wet ear
tiny closed fist
pearl
waiting
in its own dark

Love is waiting
for shell, ear, fist to open
for the poem
to dance
a slow waltz of oceans
or a crazy jiggly-headed
paper in the wind

My darling I can never have

All his desire is for another
a painless light airy place
green fields in slow motion
Words cannot hold him
he refuses my calling

Before my eyes he languishes
                              with longing
how thin the legs he swings from the bed
how matted the clots of his head

He is always walking away
down a long corridor
toward the vanishing point
of converging white walls

I am the one who survived
                    blood and knives
Why is it he carries the scars?

Car keys

A tall young man stands on the brink
of morning at the front door
of a house in the suburbs, balancing
one foot against the other
car keys held loosely
the way he holds all things

Before him stands a woman who shrinks
                           daily as he grows
She knows
he has left already
like a disappearing star in paling sky
Already scar tissue films his eyes

Arms at sides he waits for the attack
her jagged edges to pierce his thin flesh
He suffers the obligatory kiss
a quick peck down and up
then shrugs his shoulders straight
wanting escape
not wanting complications

not yet knowing the comfort of ritual
of women left, black-veiled
wailing their grief

Winter mist

I have been seeing white again

From my upstairs window the world
presents tops of things:
    crossed branches
    disconnected telephone wires
    a disembodied head
bobs like a buoy on a white sea
turns a corner and disappears
into a white whale's belly

The outline of a chimney floats
a black funnel and a grey coil snaking
Something is at home down there
something with primitive instinct
for deep and sunless places
thumps blood, churns digestive juice
               lives by lung or gill

The trick is to sew body to head
leaving no evidence of sutures
to graft branch to trunk
to ground wires with hands working
blindly beneath vapour

In winter, especially
white rises like cold foam
climbs slick steel
By late afternoon
it creeps beneath my door
seeps through the keyhole
invades my cells
occupies the spaces of my mind

Thoughts while attempting rising

Through brittle windows
a wedge of grey light enters
this winter room
still I cannot see you
the shape of your troubled breathing

outside, bare hills
and coyote's call
I think of wine-stained goblets
abandoned in the sink

these pale mornings
why can't I move from cold
hold words in the hollow of my tongue
carry them fragile as birds' eggs
into the day

on the street a car motor
turns, falters, catches
somewhere in the house a clock ticks
and clicking footsteps in the walls
announce the furnace

I think of other winters
where have the snow buntings gone

seed winter sparrows scatter
from our feeder will be green shoots
through cement
come April
when, in the green light
your bent wings might lift

Scorpion fire

November and a blue note
when out of purple dusk
the dun hills of Airdrie
amble, a camel caravan

We are a group of pilgrims
needing to travel sacred ground
to steady our uncertain course
after diversions in mistaken countries

Fretful as sick children
we want to hear our own language
not strange words written in books
structures that are monuments to our failure
a confusion of voices
towers of Babel, which, ascending
we thought to seize life
even to reach beyond
only to find ourselves braced for death

Forced to the wall we turn
circle back: the cradle
these frozen fields
their wheels of fire
like stars
in distant windows
bright spokes turning the dark
casting haloes through the mist

Our eyes strain for these signs
as our bodies remember
caves where once we were welcomed
where we crept in
out of the dusk
huddled thigh and shoulder
gnawed communal bones

Shaking loose

My old young woman's trunk
travelled skies and rivers
to meet its destiny

In the deepest corner of the basement
beneath campstove, cooler, tent
fire-blackened kettles wrapped in frangible
newspapers, it resides. Inside, cracked rattles
scuffed baby boots, a bonnet
knit with my own hands for our first born
                              pictures of people
whose names I can't remember
wearing party hats, accepting gold watches, blowing candles
all those lost occasions
and chances not taken, love letters
sifted down to the unstirred bottom

To get there I must swim a sea of long bodies
                              sprawled on couches
climb mountains of Star Treks
Pink Floyds, Blade Runners, Flames games
wade harbours of canvas boats strewn like sneakers
leap a ping-pong table
trek a desert where
the furnace like a giant condor flaps one tired wing

I open the lid and after the dust settles
plunge in my arm, pull out
artwork of early genius, unsigned but titled
                         the octopus wedding:
            he has eight arms
            thin elastics flopping
            in great clopping boots
            spastic yet managing grace
            She takes a firm stance
            on five egg carton shapes
            flowers spill from her wide arms
            smiles from her lopsided mouth

Reel in the line this day of need
sustenance to fend off cold, late afternoon, darkness
coming down, the radio predicting yet more snow

Listen to the dangle and jangle
of their beads and spangles
their fangled bangles

            flippety flip go their arms
            jogajig go their feet
            as they rise together
            out of the dry and ancient air

Saints on the prowl

like, say, alley cats
those fanatics obsessed
with cracking skeletons between their teeth
appearing ridiculous, ass high
perched on garbage can rims
tails weaving like drunken cobras
dig for fishbones to lodge in the throat
chicken splinters, snap them sharp
those loners with special slit eyes
                          to soak up the dark
night crazy for the unforgettable
taste of hunger in hollow bones
when they could have it safe
warm by air vents, milk diet, enriched
tuna snacks, choose rather
bellies churning with razors
cough up the lining
choke on the blood
starve themselves
so they can be cougars
stalk knife edges
clank tin lids
rattle desire

For the barking dogs of summer

Comes along a cruiser
dog you know is trouble
struts his colours along the avenue
In the brilliant halo of a streetlight barks his own name
dalmatian sleek and spotted or cocky cocker
docked tail, or terrier, bearded, bristly
brindled, pugnacious as a prize
fighter hating everyone

        His nose
tingles a whirl of neon
Billboards of a summer night pose vivid questions
Have you had a close shave lately?
Do you get total relief?
He cuts across the smoky haze from Louis Jack's
pricks up his ears at Mamie's wail, something about a lover
long gone, gone bad, lonesome and
shoes walking back forever and blue
guitar and young men with horns and
heartbreak hotels
        Old newspapers
travel sidewalks
rustle in vacant lots and from the Plaza
the smell of popcorn and butter

He leaves his message at the corner
post for other males on the street
fantasizes females taut for him
moves on to gardens
the most beautiful things
bones. In the night in the dark
with furious paws he digs
the soft black earth, uncovers bones
hollowed by his tongue, carved
by his teeth
         his favourite
brisket. He dreams it alive
escaping his grasp
growls with possession
as a sculptor balances the stone in his hands

A cold frame produces a garden

Once I hid between old windows
stacked against the house for winter
with coiled hose, watering can
the blown and dried leaves

Fleeing the wind, my playmates' voices
(making it home free or getting caught)
diminished and grew still and I was left
in layers out of line, frames within frames
glass on clouded glass

In silence echoing
damp and darkness falling
footsteps
        whispering on gravel
a pair of strange fuzzy feet
paused, passed, turned
passed again and again turned

Moved on
leaving me obsessed with back yards
smells of rot and worm powder
the herbal scent of leaves
late autumn's evening chill

surrounds of the fugitive life
that prowler of dusk and dreams
and doors opening for an instant
O hunter of my childhood
dragon or soft-pawed beast
oh all lost fantastical creatures
who still can break my heart

Slow fruit

Some poets envision birds
that can or cannot fly
pigeon silhouettes
the niceties of heron
                    its particularity
graceful swallows that swoop
and wheel the sun
crows unlovely as they leave
claw marks on shrieking air
flamingoes thinly balanced on one leg
Saharas of pink sand where words move like lucid grains

For some, jungles of profuse bloom
redolent, voluptuous
are there for the taking
Madagascar's lace-leaf
its intricate network of veins
can be skimmed from the surface
of transparent ponds

Others dream of snow
deserts, snout out of hard ground
shoots waiting, huddled
in the dead grass hiding

For example, the crocus
pushes up one squat flower
hairy silk petals
blinking into spring light
like a small mole emerging
　　　In April they gather
like villages of small tents
against immensity, profusely
they dot prairie grassland
open wood and thicket
their soft purple perching
with nesting meadowlarks
　　　By May the bloom
has turned to ashen grey that falls
leaving feathery silver fruit

moth wings

Plants bear flowers
fruit, without pain
the orange-breasted oriole
only has to open his throat

After harvest the moth
irresistibly drawn to lanterns
beats its delicate drum
hard on the screen

Once, on a magic night flight
by instinct the pilot
set his lights
straight into a storm
propellers slicing
spinning sleet to silver

And uncles at weddings
make music
not contained in books

Perched on chair edges
resting their chins on their fiddles
raised arms fanning the honey air
diaphanous elbows whirring

The flower girl

Arms outstretched she runs down the long street
she embraces the morning, the apple spring
blossoms pink and white sift into her hand

She disturbs nothing
as she reaches
as she bends to her basket

The women gather one by one
in loose floating robes, slippers
soundless on polished tiles
they come from inner rooms
their eyes innocent with sleep

They arrange themselves around the cloth
embroidered with golden threads
by hands of absent women
one whose love flew her into the sun
one who starved for love
one who grew twisted for love
and one, her love like cold stones
her bare feet travelled

She places the blossoms on the table
saying these are
from the highest branch
above the dust of traffic
fresh from the night

There and then they took a solemn vow
to love each other perfectly
as they spread jelly pink with fruit
containing the sun
clear of foam or sediment

But perhaps I am imagining that morning
perhaps it never happened
or, if happening, was not like that at all

I blink and she disappears
I see our short street
there are no trees
only stubbly grass
between the broken curb and the cracked sidewalk

On such a day

(no one notices a shadow in the shape of a man falling
not even an angler at the edge of the Icarian Sea)

there are no clouds
only a white gull against blue
The sun travels its ordained path between horizons

In the garden, red poppies
yellow lobelia shift in a light breeze
leaves of elm and poplar rustle

The scent of lilacs drifts through my open window

An airplane drones and disappears
from next door the swish of a broom on the walk
the drum of water into a pail

Somewhere on a leaf
a chrysalis opens
a butterfly unfolds damp wings

Sexing squash at midnight

My mother with her flashlight
tiptoes through green
voluptuous vines. Steps lightly
to protect the wide-hipped leaves
that provide her cellar fruit, glowing amber
to warm us through winter

Thick-legged, knees slightly bent
rump uplifted
she takes her stand
with sure reach plucks the bloom
the pollen trembles in her hand

Working quickly then to the finish
she folds back the petals
plunges stamen straight and true
to its mark. Flick of wrist,
the job is done, a spot of yellow
in the onion sets
poor spent shrivelled thing

Face and dress white
haloed in her own brilliant light
she stands perfectly still
and then a humming sound
and then she disappears
leaving only the afterglow
of her earthly visit

And my father's accent
forty years away
What you doin' out there, crazy woman?
doin' the job of bees. Jhee!
Bees, it seems, were scarce that year
she wouldn't take chances with her crop
crookneck, butternut, acorn, hubbard
she didn't have time during the day
so busy with canning 108 jars of green
beans, pickles, mustard and relish

To her children it is not surprising
she could pollinate in the dark
we had known such moments of her ecstasy
when, bending to us, her full breasts
hovered above our mouths like flowers

ABOUT THE AUTHOR

—

Cecelia Frey was born in northern Alberta, grew up in Edmonton and now lives in Calgary. She received a B.A. in Philosophy from the University of Alberta and, after raising a family, returned to the University of Calgary where she completed an M.A. in English. Her thesis, *Organizing Unorganized Space: Prairie Aesthetic in the Poetry of Eli Mandel,* is concerned with the impact of un-defined space on the creative consciousness.
She has worked as an editor, teacher and freelance writer and has for many years been involved in the Calgary literary community. Her short stories and poetry have been published in dozens of literary journals and anthologies as well as being broadcast on CBC radio and performed on the Women's Television Network. Numerous reviews, essays and articles have appeared in a wide range of publications including newspapers such as the *Calgary Herald* and the *Globe and Mail* and journals as varied as *Westworld* and *Canadian Literature.* Three times a recipient of the Writer's Guild of Alberta Short Fiction Award, she has also won awards for playwriting. Her fiction includes *The Nefertiti Look, The Love Song of Romeo Paquette, Salamander Moon* and *The Prisoner of Cage Farm.* Her poetry includes *the least you can do is sing, Songs Like White Apples Tasted,* and *And Still I Hear Her Singing.*

AGMV Marquis

MEMBRE DE SCABRINI MEDIA

Québec, Canada
2004